W9-BCO-497

BIG MACHINES

Diggers

David and Penny Glover

Smart Apple Media

First published in 2004 by Franklin Watts
96 Leonard Street, London EC2A 4XD

Franklin Watts Australia
45-51 Huntley Street, Alexandria, NSW 2015

Series editor: Sarah Peutrill, Designer: Richard Langford, Art director: Jonathan Hair, Illustrator: Ian
Thompson, Reading consultant: Margaret Perkins, Institute of Education, University of Reading

Picture credits: Jonathan Blair/Corbis: 6. Franklin Watts: 12t. JCB Ltd: 11c, 15b, 20, 21. Courtesy of
Komatsu Ltd: front cover, 4, 8, 12b, 14, 15t, 22. Courtesy of Orenstein-Koppel GmbH: 23. James A.
Sugar/Corbis: 10. Courtesy of Volvo Construction Equipment Ltd: 7b, 9t, 9b, 16, 17b, 18t, 18b, 19.
Woodmansterne/Picturepoint/Topham: 7t.

Published in the United States by Smart Apple Media
2140 Howard Drive West, North Mankato, Minnesota 56003

U.S. publication copyright © 2006 Smart Apple Media

Library of Congress Cataloging-in-Publication Data

Glover, David, 1953 Sept. 4-
Diggers / by David and Penny Glover.
p. cm. — (Big machines)
ISBN 1-58340-701-4
1. Excavating machinery—Juvenile literature. I. Glover, Penny. II. Title. III. Series.

TA735.G56 2005
621.8'65—dc22   2004052511

2 4 6 8 9 7 5 3

Contents

Digging holes

Diggers are big digging machines. They dig deep holes and long trenches at building sites. Diggers are also called excavators.

Pipes   **Trench**

This digger is digging a trench for underground pipes. The pipes are laid in the trench, then covered over again with soil.

Diggers sometimes do other work, too. This digger is clearing garbage from the sea.

BIG FACT

A big digger can do more in a day than hundreds of people working with picks and shovels.

VOLVO

VOLVO

VOLVO

EC140B LC

The bucket

A digger picks up a load in its bucket. The bucket is made from strong metal so that it does not bend or break as it lifts.

Bucket

This digger's bucket is picking up soil.

The bucket is shaped so that it scoops up soil as it turns on the end of the digger's arm.

VOLVO

The bucket has sharp teeth to cut into soil or even rock.

Teeth

Clamshell buckets and grapples

A digger doesn't just dig holes. The driver can change the bucket and attach a clamshell bucket or a grapple to do different jobs.

A clamshell bucket is useful for loading a pile of soil or stones onto a truck.

A clamshell bucket has two halves that bite together like a mouth.

A grapple has four or five curved spikes like long teeth. It is useful for picking up big rocks in a quarry or garbage at a dump.

Grapple

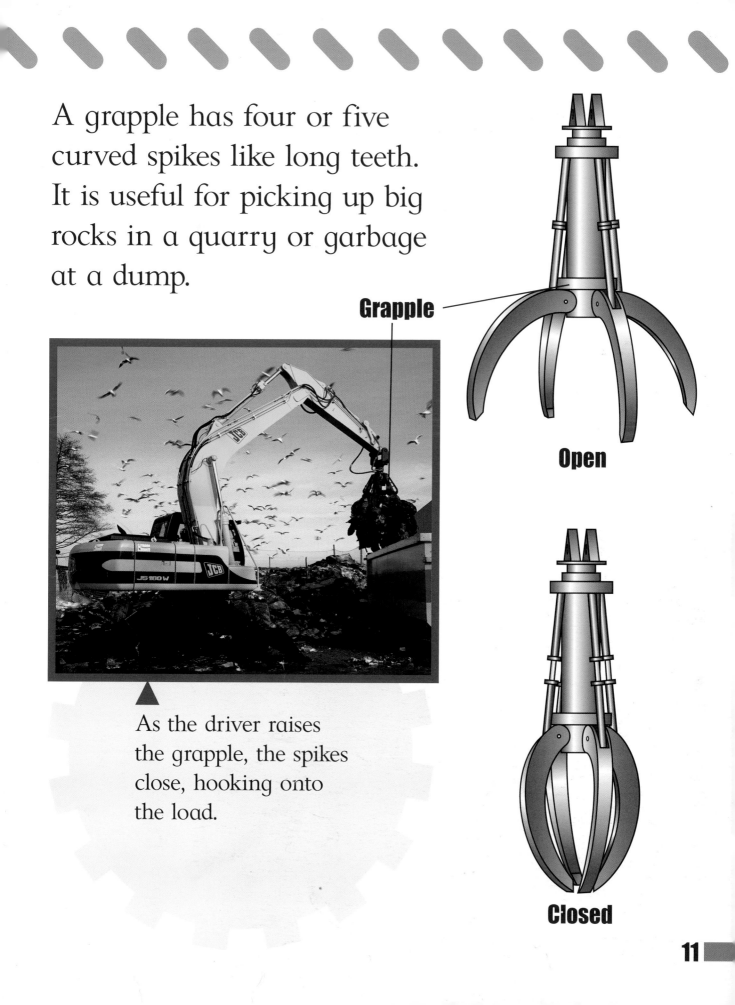

Open

As the driver raises the grapple, the spikes close, hooking onto the load.

Closed

The boom

The digger's long arm is called the boom. It swings and bends to move the bucket to where it is needed. The boom has joints like a human arm.

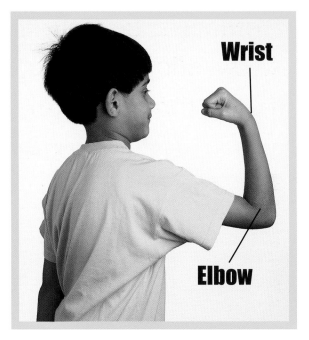

Wrist

Elbow

Hydraulic ram   Cylinder   Piston

KOMATSU

PC 290 NLC

Boom   Joint A   Joint B

Joint A works like an elbow to bend or straighten the boom.

Joint B works like a wrist. It turns the bucket to scoop up and release the load.

Your arm has muscles. A boom has hydraulic rams. Hydraulic rams make the forces that bend and straighten the joints.

Hydraulic ram

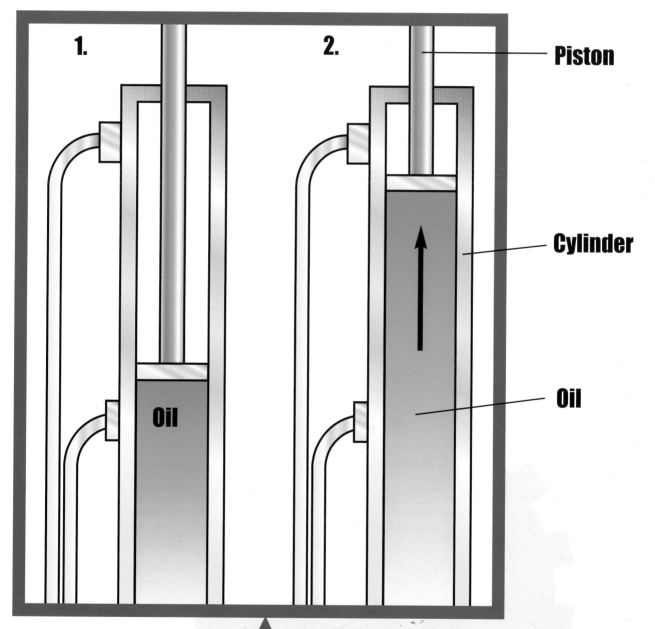

1.

2.

Piston

Cylinder

Oil

Oil

Oil fills the cylinder, pushing the piston up.

Tracks and wheels

Some diggers move around on tracks. Tracks give a good grip on rough ground. They keep the digger from slipping as it scoops up its load.

Diggers with tracks can work on steep slopes. ▶

Tracks

Each track is a loop of metal links.

Other diggers have wheels. When a wheeled digger is working, it must put down legs to keep it from slipping or tipping over.

210 NLC

Link

Legs

The engine

The engine is the part of a machine that makes it go.

A big diesel engine powers a digger.

Engine

The driver fills the fuel tank with diesel. The diesel burns inside the engine, making hot gases. These gases make the engine work.

Engine

The fuel tank on this small digger is under the driver's steps.

Step   **Fuel tank**   **Fuel tank cap**

Digger controls

The digger driver sits inside the cab. Buttons and levers work the different parts of the machine.

Cab

Two joysticks work the boom and bucket. It takes a lot of practice to drive a digger well.

Track controls

Joysticks

A digger with tracks does not have a steering wheel like a car. Two levels change the speed of the tracks.

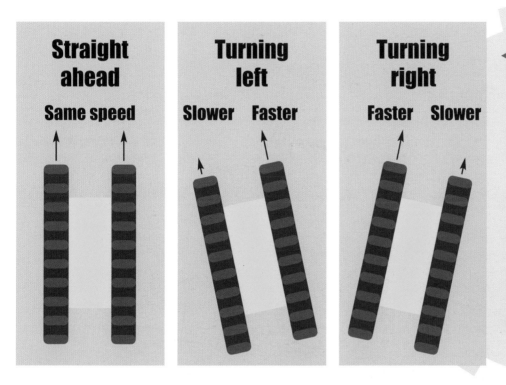

Straight ahead

Same speed

Turning left

Slower   Faster

Turning right

Faster   Slower

When both tracks move at the same speed, the digger goes in a straight line. When one track goes faster than the other, the digger turns.

Cab turning

The driver can turn the cab around to move the arm to a new place. The digger picks up a load, then swings it around to the back of a truck.

Mini-excavator

Sometimes a digging job must be done in a small space, such as a backyard. Then a mini-excavator is used.

Boom

Bucket

Tracks

This digger is about the size of a small car. But it has the same parts as the huge diggers used at large building sites.

Mini-excavators can drive through a narrow gap between two houses or turn around in a small room.

This mini-excavator is using a drill to break up a concrete floor.

Giant diggers

Giant diggers work in quarries and mines. They dig out rocks from huge holes in the ground. The rocks may contain metals and other materials.

▲ This digger uses the teeth in its giant bucket to break off the rock.

This is the biggest digger in the world. Its job is to dig up sand in Canada. The sand contains oil. The digger is called the RH400. It could pick up an ordinary road digger in its gigantic bucket.

BIG FACT

The RH400 is so big it has a break room for the crew. The room has a microwave oven, a water dispenser, a coffee machine, a refrigerator, and beds.

▲

The RH400 standing next to a normal-sized digger.

Make it yourself

Make a model digger.

You will need:

An adult to help

Paints

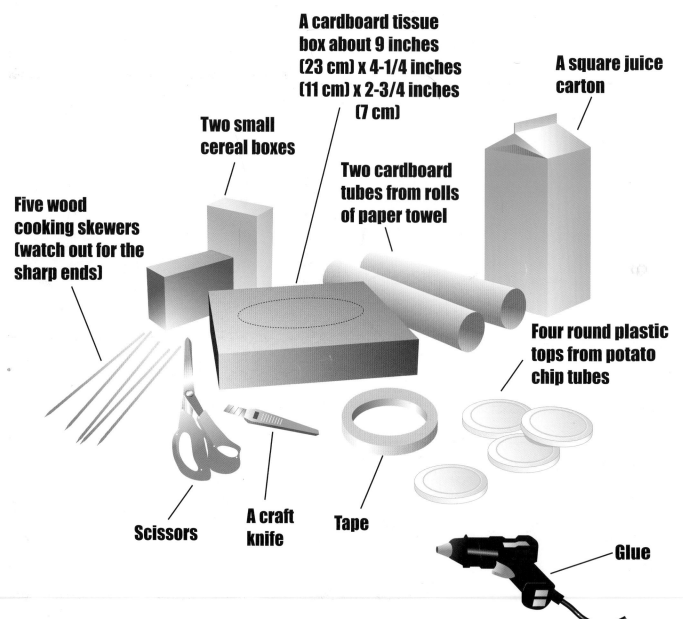

A cardboard tissue box about 9 inches (23 cm) x 4-1/4 inches (11 cm) x 2-3/4 inches (7 cm)

A square juice carton

Two small cereal boxes

Two cardboard tubes from rolls of paper towel

Five wood cooking skewers (watch out for the sharp ends)

Four round plastic tops from potato chip tubes

Scissors

A craft knife

Tape

Glue

NOTE! Get an adult to help you with the cutting and glueing.

1. Glue the cereal boxes to the tissue box to make the digger body and cab. Cut a slot about 2-1/2 inches (6 cm) x 2-1/2 inches (6 cm) at the front of the digger body.

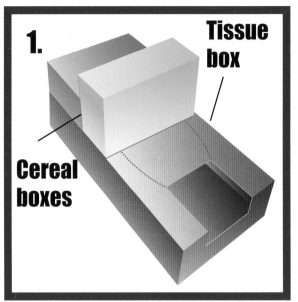

2. Cut two pieces about 2 inches (5 cm) x 1-1/2 inches (4 cm) from one end of a cardboard tube as shown.

Make holes in the tabs.

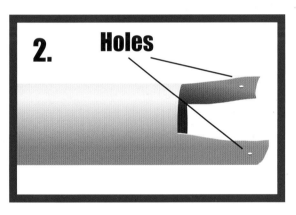

3. Make small holes in the second cardboard tube. Push the skewer through both tubes as shown. Trim the skewer to length.

This is your digger's boom.

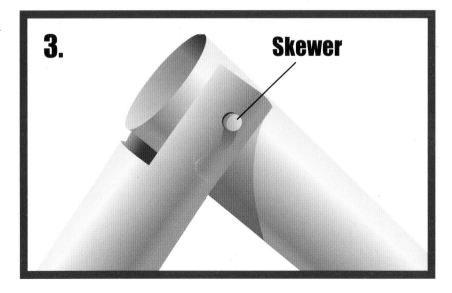

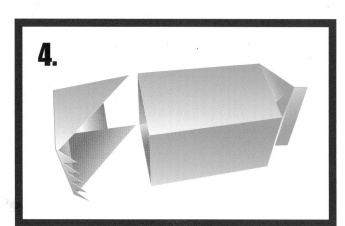

4. Cut the base from the juice carton. Use scissors to shape it into a digger bucket. Don't forget to make the teeth!

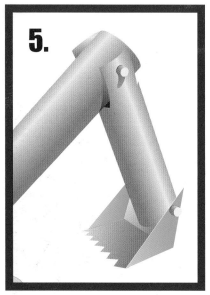

5. Attach the bucket to one end of the boom with a wooden skewer.

6. Use another skewer to attach the other end of the boom to the digger body.

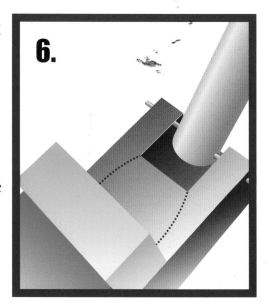

7. Push two skewers through the digger body from one side to the other to make axles.

Make holes in the round tops and push them onto the axles to make wheels. Trim the axles.

Move your digger bucket by bending the boom at its joints. Scoop up a load!

Trace your own digger

Digger words

boom

The digger's arm. The boom has joints, like an arm, that bend as the digger works.

bucket

The heavy scoop on the end of the boom. The bucket has sharp teeth to cut into soil or rock.

cab

The part of a digger in which the driver sits.

clamshell bucket

A tool like a big mouth that can pick up loads of sand and soil. A clamshell bucket can be attached to the digger in place of the bucket.

diesel

The fuel the digger engine uses to make it go.

engine
The part of a machine that burns fuel to make the forces that turn its wheels and move its parts.

excavator
Another name for a digger.

grapple
A tool made of curved spikes that can pick up large rocks and pieces of metal. A grapple can be attached to the digger in place of the bucket.

hydraulic ram
The part that pushes to bend the boom or turn the bucket. The ram is worked by oil, which pushes a piston along a cylinder.

joystick
A control like a lever for moving the boom or bucket.

tracks
The loops of metal links that some diggers have instead of wheels.

Index